for

Nan and Ollie

Emma and Gib

"And then the wind blew all your words away." — P E T R A R C H

uicksand Through the Hourglass

POEMS & DRAWINGS BY DAVE MORICE

The Toothpaste Press :: West Branch, Iowa :: December
M C M L X X X I X

Some of these poems have appeared in Bird Effort, Daily Iowan, f.p., Free Voices, Gum, Health Link, Hollow Spring Review, Interstate, Lyrical Iowa, New York Times 100 Posters, People Watcher, Roy Rogers, Search for Tomorrow, Sebastian Quill, Spirit That Moves Us, Suction, Sun & Moon, Telephone, The McKinley, and Toothpaste. Some of these poems were also published in The Actualist Anthology, 1977; *Poems*, printed by Al Buck, 1970; and *Tilt*, Toothpaste Press, 1971.

Library of Congress Data

Morice, Dave, 1946-
PS3563.087164Q5   811'.5'4   79-25714
ISBN 0-915124-28-9 signed cloth   ISBN 0-915124-27-0 pbk.

The publishers wish to thank the National Endowment for the Arts and the Iowa State Arts Council for a Small Press Assistance Grant which helped purchase materials for this book.

Contents

This Is to Signify

that you, the reader, are aware
that everything going on around you
is made possible through the cooperation
of everybody, mind you, everybody
who is involved, including
me and you, both of us.
Even though we might not be together,
we are here at the same moment
of time and space
on this very page, at this very point
in the power of language.
And you, the reader, are in control
of when and where we go
in your mind and the poem's.
You are the leader in this world.
I can only follow,
pushing for what it's worth.

Process Poem

1. Open this book.
2. Close your eyes.
3. Open your eyes.
4. Close this book.

I Am

a letter in a syllable in a word in a phrase in a clause in a
sentence in a paragraph on a page in a chapter in a story
in a collection in a dialect in a language in a society in a
culture in a civilization in a period in an epoch in a tra-
dition in an era in an age in a history in a book in a set on
a shelf in a section in a bookcase on a wall in a room in an
apartment on a floor in a building on a street in a block in
a neighborhood in a city in a county in a state in a region
in a country on a continent in a hemisphere in an ocean
on a planet in a solar system in a constellation in a galaxy
in a supergalaxy in a megagalaxy in a universe in an infini-
ty in an eternity in a reality in a dimension in an existence

Love Poem for Human Beings

When we recognize each other
How long do we have to wait

Apple

as a principle underlying the apple, the road
  contains nothing more than asphalt or cement

so we walk down the apple, figuring "this must
  be where a famous general walked and talked

about the new battle that would take place
  in the early hours of tomorrow morning."

the apple is beer. the drinkers of beer are
  satisfied with what it is, but no more than you

or I, or the tree on which the apple appears:
  lean back in the waves that the apple discharges

they make you feel as if you could think beyond
  the simple into the complex and then even further

Or as if the whole of learning were not
and the flowers, like gray hair
the hum of transparent bees
                              I was still
and too young, and you made up things besides
Shelley was young, and he made up things, too
or was it hidden, in the grass . . . What else
can you expect
or doesn't evaporate
Once again he plunges into salt
                              Salt, a sugar of sorts
Yep, the door, a weathered face, and you—sailing around
every brick in the wall
and joy was knowing of course that fish would say H i !
The seat of wisdom is really ready
and the ruddy boy lit up like a lithograph
                                        behind it all
The branches are there
to fight children
like him   And sell him dirty pictures, and bugs

Oh, so much is contained in catagories
this week, and the inarticulate sense of air, they think
Until I am twenty-eight I think I'll know
and in knowing, will care
and in caring, will sell
And one's critical sense may never
or may, who knows
and it was oft convenient to assemble
like it or not—I do!   This relates
to the problem of baking soda
Age old, on which it is contained, a plate of something
Let us affirm the real world at the expense or not
of the dry particularity
                        of air—again—air

My House

You have windows.
You have doors.
You have ceilings.
You have floors.
You have peelings.
You have sores.
You have feelings.
You have pores.

Her Little Green Book

Her little green book
is for addresses. She
takes it out, writes
my address under
the letter **M**, where
two other addresses are
already. I don't know
her name, or theirs, but
mine is third, and well
I think about it there.

18   A cigarette is a glass of milk.

A Toast to the Japanese Haiku Poets

You gather beneath the trees
Grand conversations about the leaves
Pouring out of miniature bottles
Into glasses of sound and air

Breathing in, you test the flavor
You think it, sip it, dream it, taste it
There in that corner of the woods
A thousand dialogues in a single afternoon

To you! The generous tipping of many glasses
For a decanter of wine, richer than red
For one thousand years of a stream
Winding around, goldfish swimming away

Tomorrow's Shoulder

the same thing is in the cup   coffee song
floats in the morning mist
                replacing the night with
a special coating whose antonym is sleep

as birds walk on planes, the world burns
like a star   changing its mind
& increasing the number of objects
contained within   what is the sky
really like, & does it roar?   whenever
tomorrow's shoulder bangs against
the invisible window

                                but now
are two words that work together like time
carrying you onward   to a box
you open the box   you are inside
with a picture   on fire   with love
it doesn't matter whose picture it is
unless you already know   and then you
join forces   within an invisible house
it's up in the air   it's yawning
over coffee floating in the space of a cup

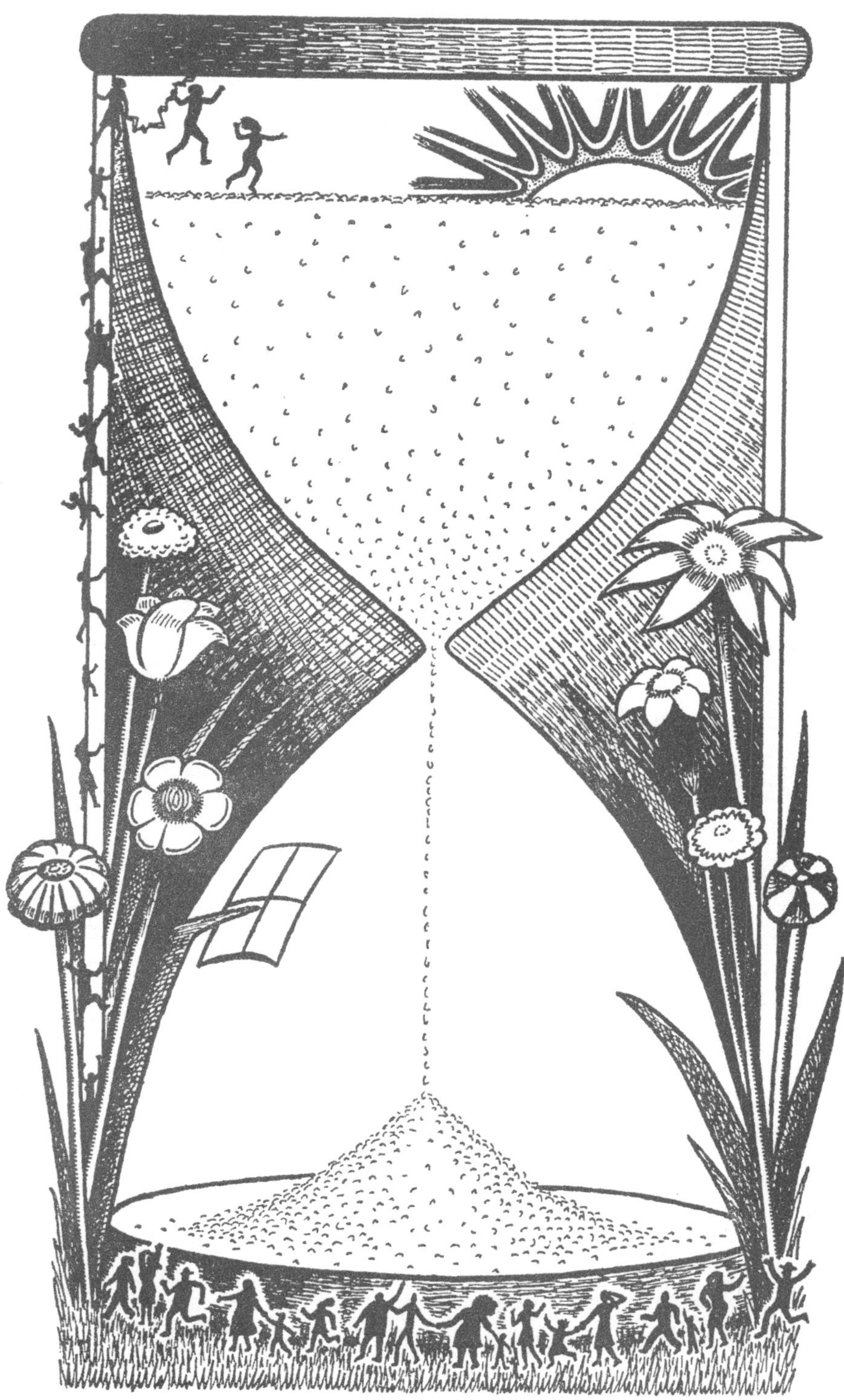

He Puts on His Hat

When he picks up his hat,
the nine planets
fly out of it.

Earth touches his left ear.
Mars touches his nose.
Jupiter, Venus, and Pluto
rest in his hair.
The other planets drift
around his arms and legs.

He puts on his hat
and walks outside.
He nods to passers-by,
for he is the solar system,
and he can't be stopped
with small talk.

22

Man Walking Dog
  for Gil

i was walking my dog in Brentwood
a couple of weeks ago, while staring at the clear
stars overhead, because the night was cool
blade after blade of grass rolled beneath our feet
we didn't pay close attention to them
till our final turn up Eulalie Ave.

the seven fence-posts that Hans, my dog, sniffed
remnants of a forgotten civilization
people who were called Americans by their friends
the full moon blinked a few times opening up
to the possibility that its craters
were eyes and wished to see us

we were Hans and me, man walking dog
a familiar archetype traveling down the field
reaching the fence, where broken yellow spokes
illuminated a historic vignette — one tricycle wheel.
no one paid much attention to us, not even the cop
who flashed the light from his squad car, then drove on

Booing Musial

sitting in the bleachers
on a hot day
a close game
going into the 8th inning

1959, my last
year in grade school
the cardinals vs the cubs
my grandmother, nan, took me

stan "the man" musial
got up to bat
with a man on first
a man on second

he struck out
on a called strike,
not swinging and missing
just mistaking

"yer out!" cried the umpire
the crowd booed
and booed, and nan
shook her head

"they shouldn't boo musial,"
she said, "he did his best."
i booed, but i thought
i was booing the umpire

Much Obliged

My grandpa used to say "much obliged"
instead of "thank you"
when someone did him a favor.

He also used to tell me
when I was in a hurry,
"Take it easy, Greasy,
you got a long way to slide!"

When he died of throat cancer,
he banged his hand on the floor
to let everyone know it was happening.

At his wake, I half-expected,
that he'd whisper to me
something like, "It's just like downtown,
only not so crowded!"

When I Worked at the Pierce Building

The construction workers assembled
the monumental St. Louis Memorial Arch
piece by piece, leg by leg, till it
connected perfectly at the top.
I watched them build
a modern pyramid. The barges
slowly trudged down river in the background.

The Bookseller

worked 12 hours today   & polished
the shelves till they sparkled   slow evening
few customers   all day long I
began, for the first time, to really enjoy
the job of bookseller   tuning in to
half-hour lunch with pay   bean soup
and salad   with fellow workers
from Iowa Book & Supply   Debi   Maria
and another, whose name remains a mystery
student asking for "Donkey's Inferno"
& Paul telling him to write his paper
with help from a manual called
"The Elephants of Style"   worn edge
of Wallace Stevens,   torn page of
the Riverside Shakespeare,   bent spine
of the quarter moon   over the roofs
here   this city   houses, like books
I ride my bike past their covers

Blanks

His mind was filled with blanks
that he'd accumulated over the years.
The first blank resulted when he forgot
what it was like to be born.
The second blank happened
when he remembered something
for the first time.
The third blank occurred
after he told someone something
that only seemed to have happened.
The next few thousand blanks
rushed past him in a flurry of images
like shoes, cities, faces, and hats
lost in the jungle of his brain.
The final blanks still exist
because they haven't yet taken place.
When they do, they'll no longer exist:
His mind will be completely
filled with blanks.

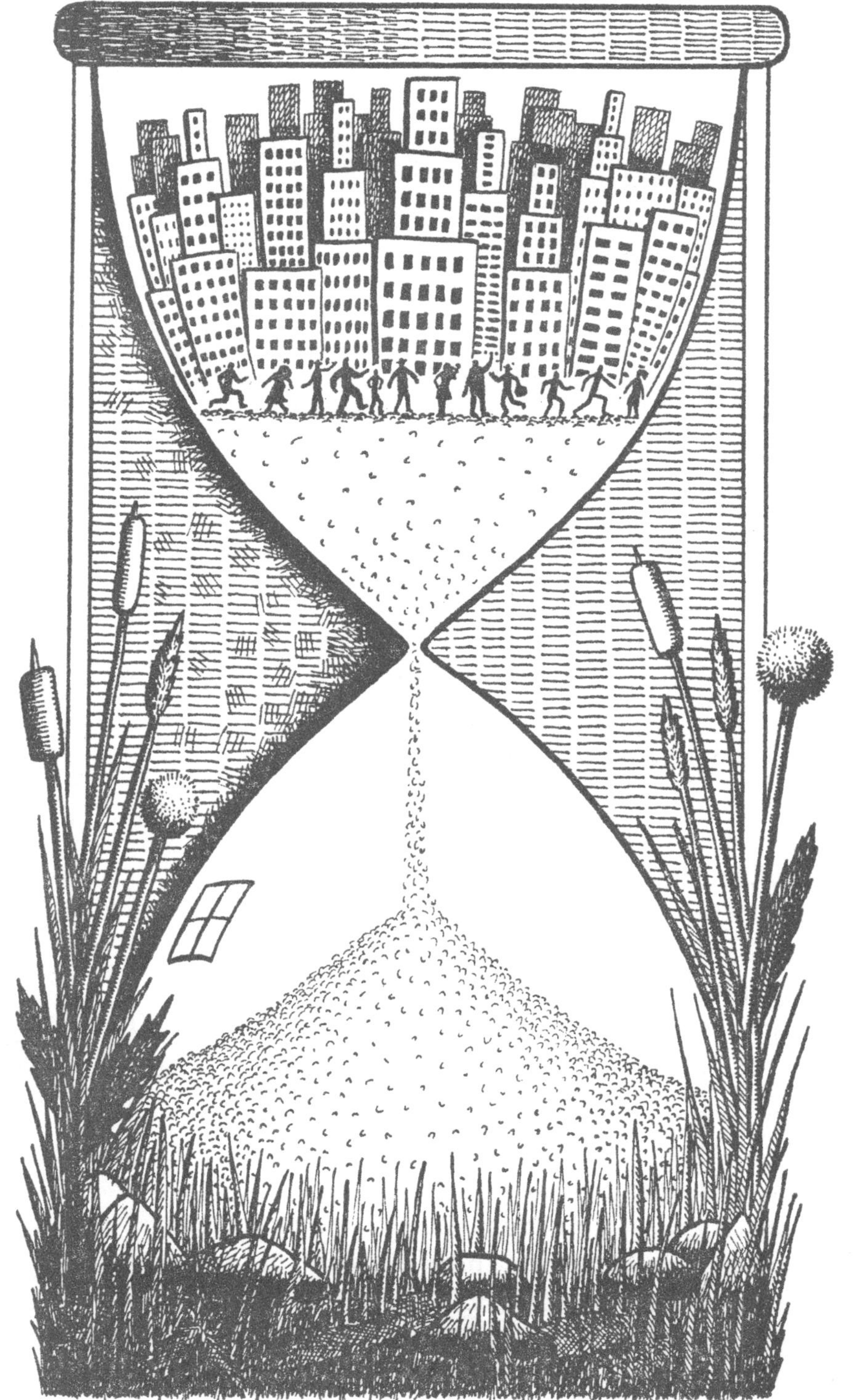

The City on Sunday

Here it is: The city
out for a stroll on Sunday,
hundreds of people zig-zagging
down the block, talking, singing,
swinging from the buildings.
It's all alive today,
in the ninety degrees of heat
melting the ice cream cones
from Baskin-Robbins across the street.
I'm seeing everything happening
as far as I'm able, with only two eyes
and one magic marker, outside
with the air so blue, the day so clear.
What a way to watch!
Sitting on a green bench
at the corner park, whose dirty bricks
and cigarette butts tremble
when the trucks go rumbling by.
O City, I want to touch you,
to be you, because you are the height
of American life, a microcosmic vision
whose flag unfurls to reveal
the people smoking, drinking,
getting stoned, and loving living.
I'm an American, like you, City,
I can't avoid or deny it,
just like I'm an earthling
with certain capacities to see myself
in mirrors of my own making.
My flag is *this*, the page.
It ain't the red, white, and blue cloth
that blows in the Courthouse wind.
It ain't the green flag of ecology
or the black flag of anarchy, either.

It's the white flag of words
that speaks for itself, that laughs or cries
about the grey flag of streets
full of dirt, tiremarks, chewing gum,
beer cans, gravel, glass,
and all the beautiful, ugly waste
of the people who decorate it every day.
O City, City, City!
You overwhelm me with your—
how can I even say
what it is, because it's
greater than the totality
of your fantastic shapes & colors.
Sitting here, I can read
your billion names in the windows,
the doors, the signs:
Morgan Optical, Cook Paint, Lind's
Frame-Up, Sweeting's Florist, Four Seasons,
Cards Et Cetera, Christian Science
Reading Room, World Radio—all
are you, the City, *this* City,
which is every American City, and more.
The sky above isn't your roof,
nor the stars, but the sky
is a start, from the point of view
that I take, gazing up.
The Jefferson Building, your tallest
architectural triumph, soars
more than eight stories into the air,
where it touches the edge of outer space.
Once I wanted to write a poem
off the top of the Jefferson Building.
I asked the owners if I could do it,
but they said no, it would be
too dangerous and would violate
the law of gravity. Still, whenever I

pass the Jefferson Building, I look up
and see a typewriter
balanced on the edge of the roof
and a long sheet of paper
inching its way down—
an epic taller than you, City,
who are taller than reality
in so many ways.
O City, I could spend my life
on this park bench, writing
about you, because there are so
infinitely many of you, and
each of you is so infinite
that every line can only be
a new beginning. I could talk about
your booze, your cars, your dope,
your men and women,
your lovers, your fighters,
your friends and foes, your
city slickers and country bumpkins;
your revolution—oh what a day
you've had in your day!
I'll speak about you over and over,
because I *am* you, My City,
but now, because you and I are here,
I'm getting up from this park bench
and I'm going to take a walk in you.

Single Solitary Heaps

waltzing across the clock
    to touch the hand of the wall
whose flower, though emotional,
    doesn't just blend in
with minus signs or rain
    But when the cat goes down
to see the practical lettuce
    his multi-colored shadow flickers:
Green fluency matches the breaks
    between the cave and the orange,
though ridges have their own
    capacity for corn cob pipes
christened "Efficiency Manual"

mabel enters the shingles,
    tests yet another glittering objective
(to open cartons of eggs)
    Pears, sanctions, febrile sheets
of sandstone, like a list too long
    to memorize—every object on earth
has to fish out its place
    and keep it for the time between
the choice and the choosing of
    "what" and "where" and "what to wear"
while the blue sky just watches
    with a blank expression
on each of its many-faceted clouds

Double Triple Quadruple Quintuple Sextuple Septuple

the bard
            the bird
                    the board
                            the beard

        far under the stars
          far under the stars
        far under the stars
          far under the stars
        far under the stars

                                    too too
            too too
                        too too
            too too
                                too too
        too too

                    musical cliff musically cleft

                        the beard
                        the board
                        the bird
                        the bard

                                too too

Hot Lights

> (written on Joyce Holland's dress
> on the Tomorrow Show, Los An-
> geles, February 11, 1974)

Thus the
soft chair
  holds
  our clothes.

  *

How many
  objects
  sit on

the table?

  *

The lines of cloth
      melt in our words!

  *

This is the
light from her hair.

  *

—The man on the phone
  needs a new fire
  so he calls Tomorrow
  to get
  the coupons.

  *

The cookies crumble into the night.

Blue Is the Symbol for Dogfish

The day of the smart umbrella is near:
When the trapazoids sleep
on their clues, a starched shirt
has too many pockets. The house wears
its shingles well, although handles
slip off the gutter and drift to
the blue shelf. Another surge,
another inkwell over the clavicle.
How earnestly the cord
connects to the backyard, able
to light up every blade of grass.
At the edge of the set, vinegar
spills on a coffee circle.
That's the chair you reach by
guiding the pool table to its cue.
Where love becomes an accordian—
why, that's where ivy
ripples in the sprinklers during
the first few days of water.
Here comes life. Take it
for its red pan of views. If weights
sew their pure, large tongues
to lick the air, you can still
stand up here at the opera.
Now and then the quality of one
is nothing compared to oil,
despite its slick spoon. The crow
cawed in the music hall, but
the only person there was gone.
Yellow, he thought, was the meaning
of ocean; and blue, he believed,
is the symbol for dogfish.

Where They Keep the Dinosaurs

Aeons ago, when the colossal beasts
of prehistory roamed the swamps and tarpits of earth,
the zoo-keepers arrived and

                              here's where
they keep the dinosaurs to this very day. As you
tour the iron and steel halls, you'll notice
how carefully the bars of the cages were carved
out of diamond. The process of converting coal
to one of the hardest materials known

                              will someday
break loose and tear through the towns of modern earth.
That will be a day to avoid, though days can't
really be avoided unless you're a heavy sleeper.
In the meantime, scientists have determined

                              they'll keep
the dinosaurs busy by building giant television sets
with reruns of Godzilla movies twenty-four hours
over and over, thus taming them so that future
generations won't have to

                              escaped and ravaged New York.
They're on their way to New Jersey. The people
have taken to the hills out of terror and a general
lack of interest in the beasts. This, of course,
frustrates them into getting even

                              more and more.
They've occupied all the major cities in the world.
Civilized people everywhere have been scattered into
small groups, for the dinosaurs have returned to
reclaim their original land, the entire planet earth.
This is the last transmission from

In the White Ruins

The goat and the shoe and the pie

And the show and the industry

And the blouses and the rooms

And the spaghetti and the noise and the wilderness

Were judging and opening and throwing

And tallying and arranging

The harsh, tall, futile, bombastic,

Green, microscopic, subtle,

Prudish, internal, big, redundant, thirsty

Buildings or crowns or

Demons or cards or elements

Or hats

Or lunch

Or Monday.

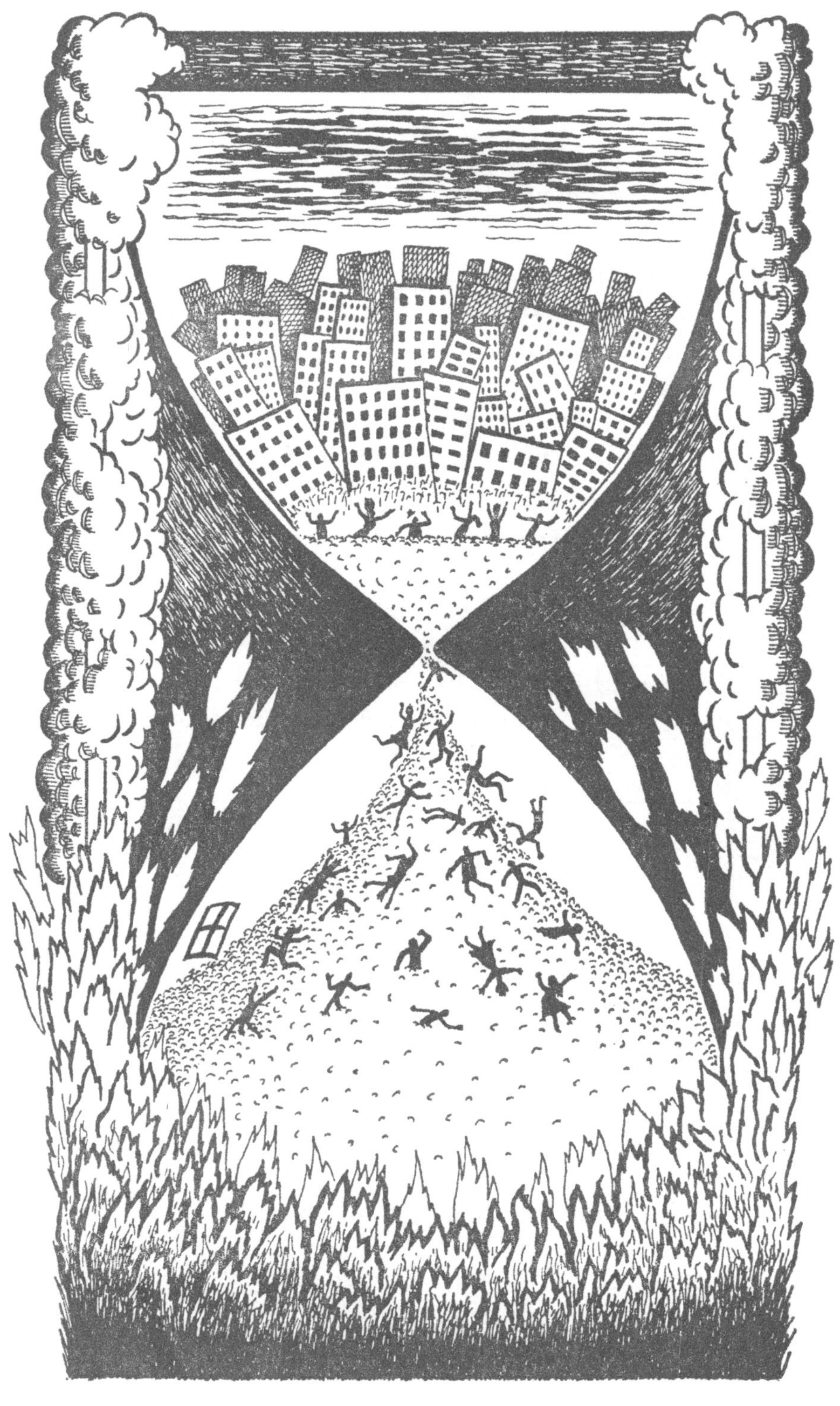

Atlantis After Hours

In a comfortable half-lit restaurant
    on the continent
            about **12,000** years ago
two young lovers
        gaze at each other
            across the table
He sips a glass
            of sweet red wine
                    twinkling in a magic moment
She brushes the hair
            out of her eyes
                    adjusts her glasses
The waiter asks,
        "Will there be anything else?"
    The band blasts the latest songs
                on solar-powered guitars, piano,
                        and drums
    Ancient rhythms
                shake the ocean floor
The man takes the woman's hand
                and replies,
                    "That'll be all, thank you."
    They pay the check
                leave a generous tip
                        and exit through
                            the pneumatic doors
        "It's a wonderful night," she whispers
                in his ear
He smiles, kisses her lightly on the cheek
            "It always is
                    when we're together," he murmurs
        confident that their love
                                is eternal

Looms of Drats

Looms of drats flyin' around
Cantation-like in the gilt dark
Where we trail each other
Off, going here, around there

But when the sun makes us shop
For more wild wigs like Veronica
We rub noses with the hobnobs
As the cactus clicks in the cup.

Yes, we do. We're here.
We've got nothin' not to do.
So we don't do it without.
Veronica turns around, styles herself.

And shh the wave drives on and on
At the ocean's edge, like lotion,
Or motion, and the slingshot divine
At the ocean's edge, like lotion.

Looms of drats flyin' around
But when the sun makes us shop
Yes, we do. We're here.
And shh the wave drives on and on

The Honeymoon

Pow!   I love you

and that's all I remember of you

another door this time

where's the paperboy

she's an ex hindu   but she doesn't

know how

to be   What?   Corned beef?

this is a wonderful party   this is poetry

the hard sell

I remember how incredibly dull a brutal mistress can be

every night now

who walks through thought

The Babies

the babies
laid their teeth
on the edge of the sandbox

the happy dish
came along
and gathered them up

their mothers
saw it happening
from the window's window

shrieking, they pulled
the babies
down like venetian blinds

Smile

When I entered the tavern,
the gusty wind behind me
slammed the door on my heels.
The bartender smiled, saying
"Wind does that in these parts.
Wind and love." I smiled,
seeing that he was smiling.
  His smile was bigger than mine,
so I pulled mine apart with
both hands to increase its size.
It tore, however, leaving
two rips in my cheeks, and
a couple of ribbons of blood
streaming down my neck. I
could feel the wind on my neck.
Someone had opened the door.
  I looked. I tried to smile.
My cheeks tore open further,
all the way to my ears. I
heard them rip very clearly.
The bleeding increased. My shirt
was stained with two red stripes
that looked like suspenders.
  I decided to leave. I looked
funny. People were laughing
at my huge smile. I leaned back
and laughed heartily. I heard
someone say, as my mouth ripped
further, "Wind does that
in these parts. Wind and love."

The Iowa City Late-at-Night
After-the-Bars-Close Blues

There was beer and friends
In front of me
But now I'm sitting
In my tree

My room, that is
It's where I go
My radio's playing
An all-night show

The woods surround me
The town, that is
It's silent now
Where beer once fizzed

The lights are out
They've blown a fuse
It's the Iowa City Late-at-Night
After-the-Bars-Close Blues

The world of people
Spins through the night
While the universe
Is off to the right

To the left, the earth
Spins on and on
Like an empty bottle
Tossed on the lawn

The stars are out
They can't refuse
The Iowa City Late-at-Night
After-the-Bars-Close Blues

it rang

and as it rang

I listened

and as I listened

I heard

and as I heard

I saw

and as I saw

the moon

and as the moon

I dialed

and as I dialed

the ring

and as the ring

I watched

and as I watched

it rang

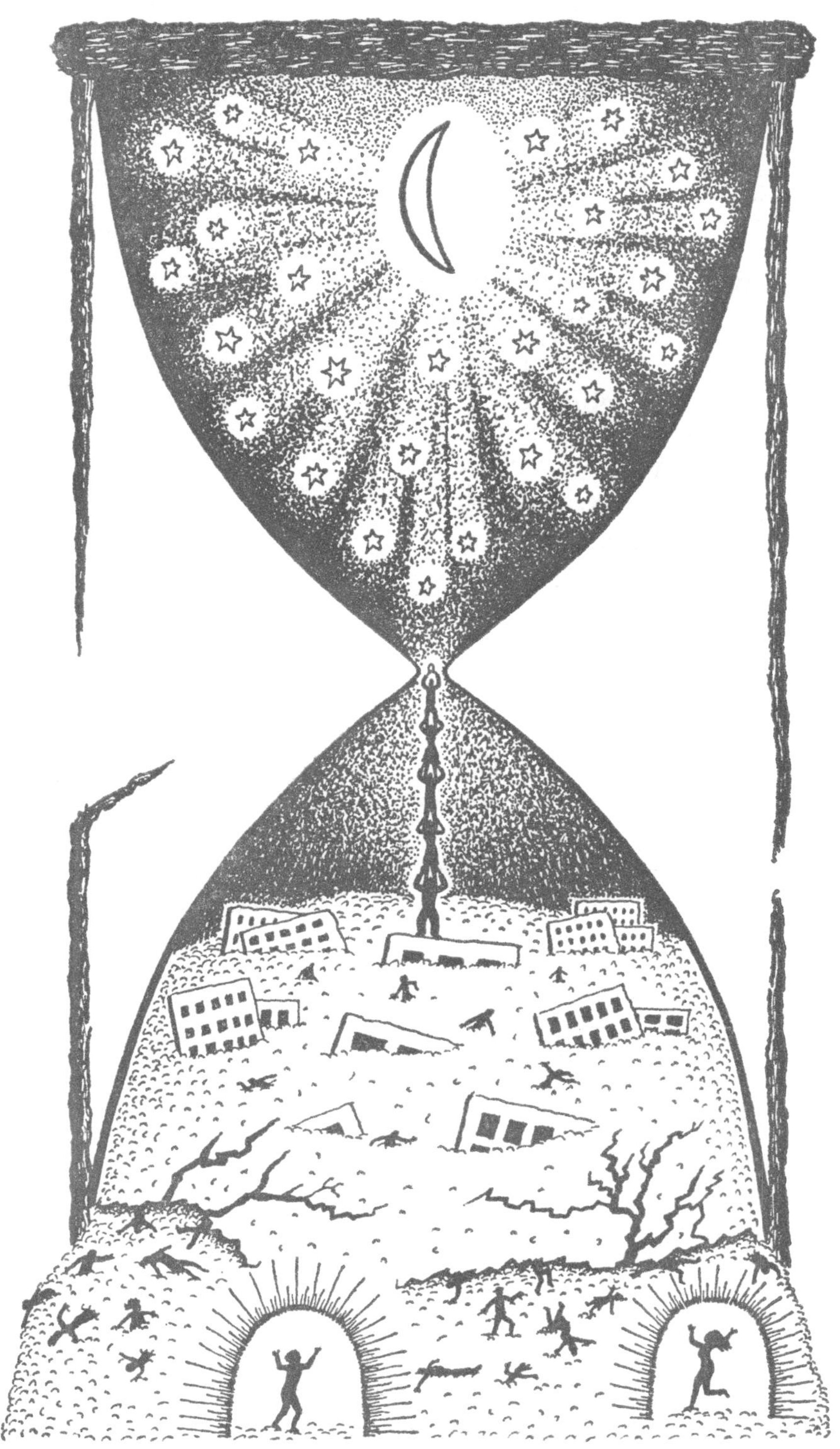

It's the right arm
pouring coffee
for the left mouth to drink,
  O Ulysses
  whose feet climb walls
   till the ceiling
issues its proclamation
  to the customers:

  "Tonite the moon
   will be eclipsed
    by the earth.
  Tonite will really be night!"

  As it happens,
   I sit here drinking coffee
   too wrapped up
    in the atmosphere
     to gaze at the moon.

The 95-year-old poet
  walks in and says,

"You can meet her in music,
  You can meet her in poems,
  But the best thing of all
   Is to meet her alone."

  Ah, the wisdom
   that comes with age
    is so often like
    the wisdom
    that comes
    with youth . . .

   I'm talking about you, sir,
who sat down in the booth up front.

Do you relish the fact that
you could've been another
        Adolph Hitler or Jesus Christ.
Instead you chose to be you,
    a unique individual,
sometimes a hero,
    sometimes a heel.

At least,
    when you die,
    they'll be able to put on your tombstone:

        "He, too, was human."

    Oh, that's in the future,
        so don't hold your breath.
    Who knows? Maybe
    you're the one we've been waiting for,
        the person for whom no epitaph
            will ever be written.

    "You're missing the eclipse."
Which doesn't seem likely,
since my shadow is contributing
    to the blackout up there
as much as anyone's.

    White lightening!
        I see you,
        everybody,
        at the end of the trail.
    Your horses are neighing
        and pulling at the reins.
    You wait in a pyramid
        covered with neon.
Something tells you
    that something's moving
through the underbrush.

"You" is a memory
        falling through oblivion
as your horses ride off into the sunset.
        "I" is a dream
            whose dreamer
            woke, not up, but out.

    Think —
            no thoughts come.
    Talk —
            no talk comes.
    Walk —
            who's walking
                these days?

The guy from Missouri
    wanted some money
                but he didn't notice
            that the sky was cloudy.
        When it rained,
            he was so surprised
        that he went broke.
    He's still there,
        a monument to water.

        The people of earth
    call him names
            because he stands
                for everyone.
    An apple
        drifts
        through a tear:
            He doesn't even blink,
        he's that spontaneous.
It rains some more:
    He weeps like a cloud
            disappointing

                    the weatherman.
The giant camera
        takes his picture
           to the moon.
The ashtray
        sits
           on his atomic structure,
     where cigarettes
           do a little square-dance
     to the apocalypse,
           which, by the way,
     is as natural
              as that crowd
           handing out leaflets.

Here in the wheel,
     the year 1975
rolls down the street,
          picking up momentum
     and shooting off sparks.
When it reaches
          the Hamburg Inn,
Odysseus will be
          waiting outside.
He'll stick out his thumb
          and hitch a ride.

The No-Parking Sign

in the non-light
of an overcast day,
the no-parking sign
has no shadow

no car parks under it
where no driver sits
smoking no cigarette
waiting for no one

no, he is free, completely
free to go nowhere
screeching no wheels
in no cloud of dust

he is not there, and he
will not stay, because
he does nothing: he obeys
the no-parking sign

In Memory of W.H. Auden

I didn't know you died
till a week or so later
when Allan Kornblum told me
that he played your poetry record
at an open reading
at the Sanctuary, an Iowa City bar.
I made the posters
for that event, well-attended
I'm told, but I couldn't go
because I had bronchitis
and took antibiotics and codeine.
I heard you read in person
seven years ago at St. Louis U's gym.
That was the first poetry reading
I ever went to, and I was
deeply impressed, especially when
the microphone buzzed
and blew a fuse. You pushed it
away and angrily shouted
DAMN THING! and everyone
thought that was funny,
but you were really pissed.
At this time I still don't know
how you died, or exactly when.
I'm sorry it happened
to you as well as Ezra
Pound, who died a few months ago,
and Pablo Neruda, who passed
away a few days before you.
I always pictured Pound
as a deposed monarch, Neruda
as a surrealistic king,
and you as a real, live poet.

(6/14/79)
  for Bobbi Nowland

we walk
home

by fol-
lowing

the trees
down

a dark
corridor

of leaves
and

branches to
kiss

beneath every
now

and then
again

Little Semi-Colons of the Night

the dew-lit street
with two moths
circling

;

dog barks
& chases
barks
chases

;

silver Pinto's
engine dies
at each stop

;

after 4:00
& I have
a tire
in my back

The Second Last Myth

The people walked out of the room of water
into the room of air
and sat down in a circle of rocks.
The oldest in the group
pointed at the clouds:
There were leaves among the clouds.
"I see the gates, the doors,"
said one of the younger people.
Another said, "I see the windows
that've replaced the sky!"
They stood up.
The old ones looked out the windows
and tried to open the gates and the doors.
The young ones climbed trees,
ate the leaves,
inhaled the clouds.

Cowboys

                        for Lil

all

                of us
   are here
                roped in
by lariats of sleep
      This is a dream
I am the dreamer

         I have the advantage

This book was designed, handset, and printed by Allan
Kornblum. The text was set in Bulmer types, and printed
on Curtis Rag paper on an ATF Little Giant. The initial
Q was cut in wood by Al Buck; the drawings were photo-
engraved at Pella Engraving. The Q and drawings were
printed on a hand-fed Challenge-Gordon platen press. Of
the 1,100 copies in the edition, 100 were numbered and
signed by the author and cased in cloth at the Black Oak
Bindery; 1,000 copies were smyth sewn and glued into
Strathmore wrappers at Prairie Fox.